HOLT SCIENCE & TECHNOLOGY

ASSESSMENT CHECKLISTS & RUBRICS

HOLT, RINEHART AND WINSTON

A Harcourt Education Company

Orlando • Austin • New York • San Diego • Toronto • London

To the Teacher

This booklet contains a wide array of assessment-related checklists and rubrics to help you be more effective and efficient in your assessment of student progress and comprehension. Over 45 individual checklists are included in this booklet to provide you with a variety of options to fit your particular teaching preferences. You will find checklists and rubrics that are teacher centered as well as some that are designed for students to use in assessing their own work. You will even find checklists that are designed to direct and support self-assessment of cooperative groups. Checklists are also provided to monitor student progress, Portfolios, and ScienceLogs. Scan the Contents, pages iii–iv, to get a quick overview of the types of checklists and rubrics available in this handy booklet.

Customize with the One-Stop Planner CD-ROM!

All of the checklists and rubrics in this booklet, and *more,* can be found on the *One-Stop Planner CD-ROM*. This CD-ROM not only allows for convenient storage of a large number of checklists and rubrics but also allows for complete customization to fit specific needs. Although most of the checklists and rubrics contain predetermined criteria, you can change any or all of them quickly and easily. Using the *One-Stop Planner CD-ROM,* you can create your own forms that include not only your own criteria but also your students' names and other pertinent information.

Front Cover Photo Credits (z), Pete Carmichael/Getty Images; (arch), Steve Niedirf Photography/Getty Images; (aircraft), Creatas/PictureQuest; (owl), Kim Taylor/Bruce Coleman

Printed in the United States of America

ISBN 0-03-035204-5   2 3 4 5 6 023 09 08 07 06 05

▪CONTENTS▪

TEACHER ASSESSMENT CHECKLISTS

PROGRESS REPORTS

Name _____ Date _____ Class _____

Group Evaluation of Cooperative Group Discussion

Scoring Key:	**Group:** _____
2 All members	**Unit/Chapter:** _____
1 Some members	**Activity:** _____
0 No members	

_____ We each contributed to the discussion.

_____ We questioned each other's ideas.

_____ We were willing to have our own ideas questioned.

_____ We showed respect for each other's ideas.

_____ We listened to each other without interrupting.

_____ We modified our views when faced with new ideas.

_____ We helped to involve every member of the group in the discussion.

_____ We stayed focused on the topic.

_____ We got along well.

_____ We showed interest in and enthusiasm for the discussion.

We acquired the following ideas as a result of the discussion:

_____

_____

We could improve our discussion by:

_____

Signature of group members: _____ _____

Date: _____ _____ _____

_____ _____

Teacher Comments: _____

_____

Signature: _____ **Date:** _____

Name _____ Date _____ Class _____

Self-Evaluation and Peer Evaluation of Cooperative Group Discussion

Scoring Key:	Group: _____
2 Often	Unit/Chapter: _____
1 Sometimes	Activity: _____
0 Never	

In the second column, I have put check marks beside at least three items that I have chosen to evaluate today. In the columns to the right, I have scored my performance on these items and the performance of each of the members of my group.

Skill	Evaluated	Me			
Contributed information and ideas to the discussion					
Questioned the ideas of others					
Was willing to have ideas questioned					
Showed respect for the ideas of others					
Listened to others without interrupting					
Modified views when faced with new ideas					
Helped involve everyone in the discussion					
Helped the group stay focused on the topic					
Got along well with all group members					
Showed interest and enthusiasm					

Here are some suggestions to make our group work better.

_____

Name _____ Date _____ Class _____

About My Portfolio

Complete the following statements for each contribution to your Portfolio.

_____

This contribution was done as part of the following assignment:

_____

_____

_____

_____

I chose to include this work in my Portfolio because:

_____

_____

_____

_____

Doing this assignment has helped me:

_____

_____

_____

_____

My favorite part of this assignment was:

_____

_____

_____

_____

Other comments:

_____

_____

_____

_____

Portfolio Self-Evaluation

Read the criteria below. Then use the numbers given in the key to reflect the strengths and weaknesses of your Portfolio. Write the number that most honestly reflects your personal assessment of your Portfolio.

Scoring Key:

5 **Excellent**

4 **Good**

3 **Average**

2 **Needs Improvement**

1 **Poor**

Criteria	Rating
1. My Portfolio contains all of the items required by my teacher.	
2. My Portfolio demonstrates my overall improvement in science.	
3. My Portfolio demonstrates my knowledge of the unit.	
4. My Portfolio demonstrates my ability to see relationships among topics and concepts in science.	
5. My Portfolio demonstrates my ability to solve problems.	
6. My Portfolio demonstrates my ability to think critically.	
7. My Portfolio demonstrates my ability to communicate effectively about ideas learned in this unit.	
8. My Portfolio demonstrates my ability to use science process skills.	

Explanation of the Ratings

Explain why you deserve the ratings that you chose. For example, you might want to identify one or more items in your Portfolio that support your rating.

Criteria	Reasons for Rating
1.	
2.	
3.	
4.	
5.	
6.	
7.	
8.	